For my Uncle Vicente, Aunt Reginalda, Aunt María,
Aunt Delfina, and all my relatives and friends from Atoyac,
the beloved town of my childhood. — F.X.A.

Para mi tío Vicente, tía Reginalda, tía María,
tía Delfina y todos mis parientes y amigos de Atoyac,
ese querido pueblo de mi infancia. — F.X.A.

For Wendi/Para Wendi. — M.C.G.

The title of this book refers to Mexico-Tenochtitlan, the fabulous city founded by the Aztecs in 1325, on a small island in the middle of Lake Texcoco. The Aztec name for this city (Mexico) comes from *metztli* (moon), *xictli* (bellybutton), and *o* (from). I can envision this ancient city gleaming as if it were the bellybutton of the moon reflected in the lake.   —*Francisco X. Alarcón*

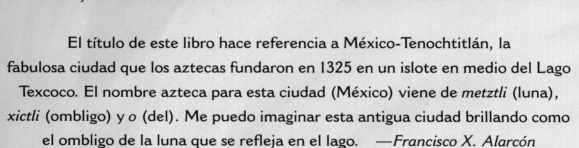

El título de este libro hace referencia a México-Tenochtitlán, la fabulosa ciudad que los aztecas fundaron en 1325 en un islote en medio del Lago Texcoco. El nombre azteca para esta ciudad (México) viene de *metztli* (luna), *xictli* (ombligo) y *o* (del). Me puedo imaginar esta antigua ciudad brillando como el ombligo de la luna que se refleja en el lago.   —*Francisco X. Alarcón*

Poems copyright © 1998 by Francisco X. Alarcón. All rights reserved.
Pictures copyright © 1998 by Maya Christina Gonzalez. All rights reserved.
Editor: Harriet Rohmer   Design and Production: Cathleen O'Brien   Editorial/Production Assistant: Laura Atkins
Thanks to the staff of Children's Book Press: Sharon Bliss, Shannon Keating, Janet Levin, Stephanie Sloan,
Emily Romero, and Christina Tarango. And thanks to David Schecter for his editorial help.

Distributed to the book trade by Publishers Group West.
Quantity discounts are available through the publisher for educational and nonprofit use.

Library of Congress Cataloging-in-Publication Data
Alarcón, Francisco X., 1954-
From the bellybutton of the moon and other summer poems / poems, Francisco X. Alarcón ; illustrations, Maya Christina
Gonzalez = Del ombligo de la luna y otros poemas de verano / poemas, Francisco X. Alarcón ; ilustraciones, Maya Christina
Gonzalez. p.   cm.
Summary: A bilingual collection of poems in which the renowned Mexican American poet revisits and celebrates his child-
hood memories of summers, Mexico, and nature.   ISBN 0-89239-153-7
1. Children's poetry, American. 2. Children's poetry, American—Translations into Spanish. 3. Summer—Juvenile poetry.
4. Mexico—Juvenile poetry. [1. Summer—Poetry. 2. Nature—Poetry. 3. Mexico—Poetry. 4. American poetry—Mexican
American authors. 5. Mexican American poetry (Spanish). 6. Spanish language materials—Bilingual.] I. Gonzalez, Maya
Christina, ill. II. Title. PS3551.L22F76 1998 811'.54—dc21 97=37457 CIP AC

Printed in Singapore by Tien Wah Press, Ltd.
10   9   8   7   6   5   4

Children's Book Press is a nonprofit publisher of multicultural and bilingual literature for children,
supported in part by grants from the California Arts Council. Thanks to the Charles Schwab
Corporation Foundation for their contribution toward the publication of this book.
Write us for a complimentary catalog:
Children's Book Press, 246 First Street, Suite 101, San Francisco, CA 94105.
cbookpress@cbookpress.org

DATE DUE   c.1

15.95

From the Bellybutton of the Moon

and Other
Summer Poems

of the Moon

Del Ombligo

y otros
poemas de verano

de la Luna

Poems/Poemas   Francisco X. Alarcón

Illustrations/Ilustraciones   Maya Christina Gonzalez

Children's Book Press/Libros para niños
San Francisco, California

Blue

I face south
  "blue" I cry

same color—
  the sea, the sky

Azul

miro al sur
  grito "azul"

un color:
  cielo y mar

Green Grass

we love
to go shoeless
on green grass

Mother Earth
loves to tickle
our bare feet

Hierba verde

nos gusta
andar descalzos
entre la hierba verde

a la Madre Tierra
le encanta hacernos
cosquillas en los pies

Niebla del monte

tierno
aliento
de montañas

vaho
juguetón
que nubla

las ventanas
de la panadería
del pueblo

los anteojos
de oro
de mi padre

el parabrisas
de la camioneta
familiar

cuando cruzamos
la Sierra Madre
Occidental

Mountain Mist

tender
breath
of mountains

playful
steam
clouding

the windows
of the village
bakery

the golden
eyeglasses
of my father

the windshield
of my family's
station wagon

as we cross
Mexico's western
mountain range

1. From the Bellybutton of the Moon
Del ombligo de la luna

cuando	whenever
digo	I say
"México"	"Mexico"
siento	I feel
en la cara	the same wind
el mismo viento	on my face
que sentía	I felt when
al abrir	I would open
la ventanilla	the window
en mi primer	on my first
viaje al sur	trip south
en coche	by car
veo	I see
otra vez	Atoyac
Atoyac	again
el pueblo	the town
donde se crió	where my mother
mi madre	was raised
y yo pasé	and I spent
vacaciones	summer
de verano	vacations
oigo	I hear
voces	familiar
familiares	voices
risas	laughter
saludos	greetings
despedidas	farewells
huelo	I smell
las gardenias	my grandma's
de mi abuela	gardenias

2. From the Bellybutton of the Moon
Del ombligo de la luna

cuando	whenever
digo	I say
"México"	"Mexico"
oigo	I hear
a mi abuela	my grandma
hablándome	telling me
de los aztecas	about the Aztecs
y de la ciudad	and the city
que fundaron	they built
en una isla	on an island
en medio	in the middle
de un lago	of a lake
"México"	"Mexico"
me dice	says
mi abuela	my grandma
"significa:	"means: from
del ombligo	the bellybutton
de la luna"	of the moon"
"no olvides	"don't forget
tu origen	your origin
mijo"	my son"
quizás	maybe
por eso	that's
mismo	why
cuando	whenever
ahora digo	I now say
"México"	"Mexico"
quiero	I feel
tocarme	like touching
el ombligo	my bellybutton

Girasol

algo
de flor
algo
de sol

Sunflower

somewhat
a flower
somehow
a sun

Morning Yolks

Auntie Reginalda
always served us
delicious breakfasts—
little yellow suns
smiling in our plates

Yemas matutinas

mi tía Reginalda
siempre nos servía
unos ricos desayunos:
pequeños soles amarillos
que en platillos se sonreían

13

Antigua sabiduría

después
de trabajar
todo el día

como
campesino
de sol a sol

ordeñando
vacas
dormilonas

lavando
limpiando
dando de comer

a todos los animales
los chiquitos
y los grandotes

reparando
cercas
acequias

escardando
regando
su maizal

mi tío Vicente
descansando por fin
en su mecedora

muy calmado
bajo las estrellas
nos decía:

"mañana
empezamos
todo de nuevo"

Ancient Wisdom

after
working
all day

as a farmer
from dawn
to dusk

milking
sleepy
cows

washing
cleaning
feeding

all the animals
the small ones
and the big ones

repairing
fences
waterways

weeding
watering
his cornfield

Uncle Vicente
finally resting
in his rocking chair

would tell us
very calmly
under the stars:

"tomorrow
we'll start
all over".

Mariposa

Mariposa
se llama
mi vaca
consentida

porque tiene
una mariposa
marcada
en la cara

¡qué maravillosa
la mariposa
de mi vaca
Mariposa!

sus grandes
ojos redondos
le salen
de las alas

¡cómo le gusta
oler las flores
que encuentra
en su camino!

las mariposas
del campo
revoloteando
la siguen

quizás
más que vaca
¡de veras es
una mariposa!

Sol de verano

luminosa
naranja
colgada
del árbol
del mediodía

Mariposa is the Spanish word for butterfly.

Summer Sun

luminous
orange
hanging
from the tree
of noontime

Mariposa

Mariposa
is the name
of my favorite
cow

because she has
the mark
of a butterfly
on her face

how wonderful
the butterfly
on my cow
Mariposa!

her big
round eyes
come through
the wings

how she loves
to smell the flowers
she finds along
her path!

the butterflies
of the fields
fluttering
follow her

perhaps
more than a cow
she really is
a butterfly!

17

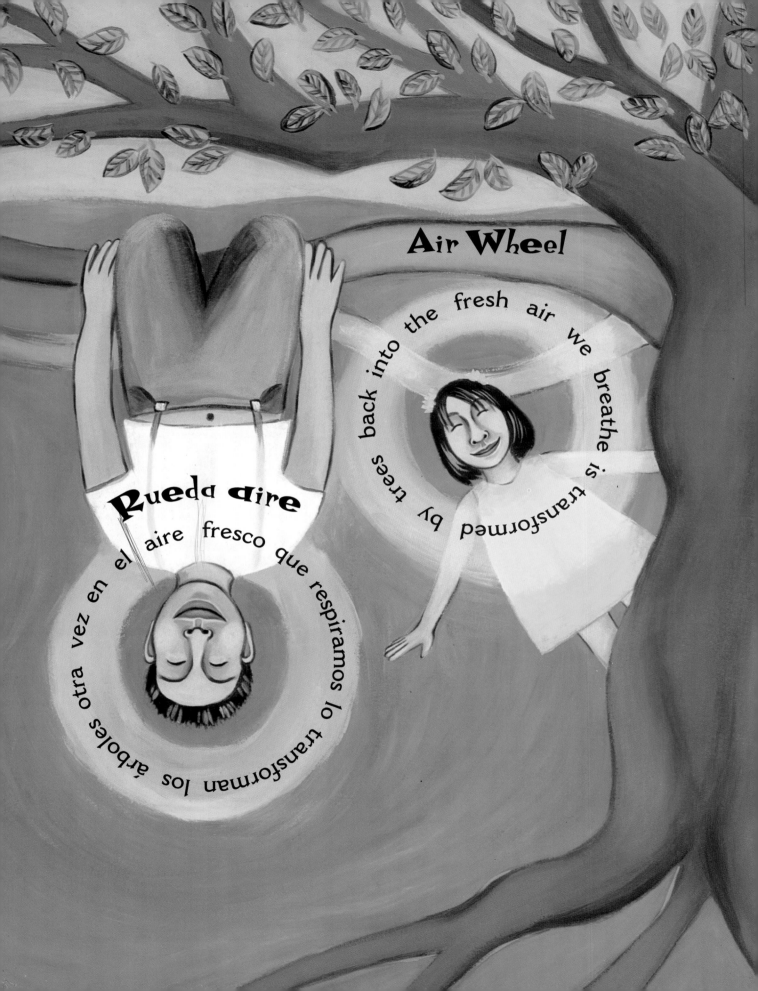

Air Wheel

back into the fresh air we breathe is transformed by trees

Rueda aire

otra vez en el aire fresco que respiramos lo transforman los árboles

Water Wheel

lakes rivers sea water sun mist clouds rain snow mountains

Rueda agua

lagos ríos mar agua sol vapor nubes lluvia nieve montañas

19

Ducha diaria

Daily Shower

en el verano	during
llueve	summer
a cántaros	it pours
todos los días	every day
a las cinco	at five
en punto	on the dot
toda la gente	everybody
busca resguardo	takes cover
pero pronto	but soon
se despeja	it clears up
y de nuevo	and the sun
sale el sol	comes back
las calles	streets
las aceras	sidewalks
brillan de	shine so neat
tan limpias	and clean
después	after
de tomar	taking
su ducha	their daily
diaria	shower

20

Rainbow

with seven
ribbons
of colors

the Earth
rewards
the Sky

Arco iris

con siete
listones
de colores

la Tierra
premia
al Cielo

Island

every island
dreams

of being
a continent

Isla

toda isla
sueña

con ser
un continente

Mar

tus olas

se ríen

a carcajadas

22

Question

can question marks
by any chance
really be
little seahorses?

Pregunta

¿son los puntos
de interrogación
acaso en realidad
caballitos del mar?

Sea

your waves

burst out

laughing

Las llaves del universo

Keys to the Universe

mi abuelito
Pancho
nos enseñó

my Grandpa
Pancho
taught us

a mis hermanos
mis hermanas
y a mí

my brothers
my sisters
and me

las primeras
letras
en español

our first
letters
in Spanish

su sala
de estar fue
nuestro salón

his living
room was
our classroom

"y éstas son
las meras llaves
del universo"

"and these are
the true keys
to the universe"

nos decía
apuntando
a las letras

he'd tell us
pointing to
the letters

del alfabeto
en el improvisado
pizarrón

of the alphabet
on the makeshift
blackboard

Bilingüe

en casa
tenemos
un perro
bilingüe

"guau guau"
saluda
primero
en español

en caso
que no lo
entiendan
entonces

"bow wow"
repite
ladrando
en inglés

26

Bilingual

at home
we have
a bilingual
dog

"guau guau"
he first
greets you
in Spanish

and in case
you don't
understand
him then

"bow wow"
he repeats
barking
in English

Wind

at night
you make
trees
whisper

Viento

de noche
tú haces
susurrar
a los árboles

28

We Are Trees

our roots
connect

with the roots
of other trees

our branches
grow wanting

to reach out
to other branches

Somos árboles

nuestras raíces
se comunican

con las raíces
de otros árboles

nuestras ramas
crecen deseando

otras ramas
alcanzar

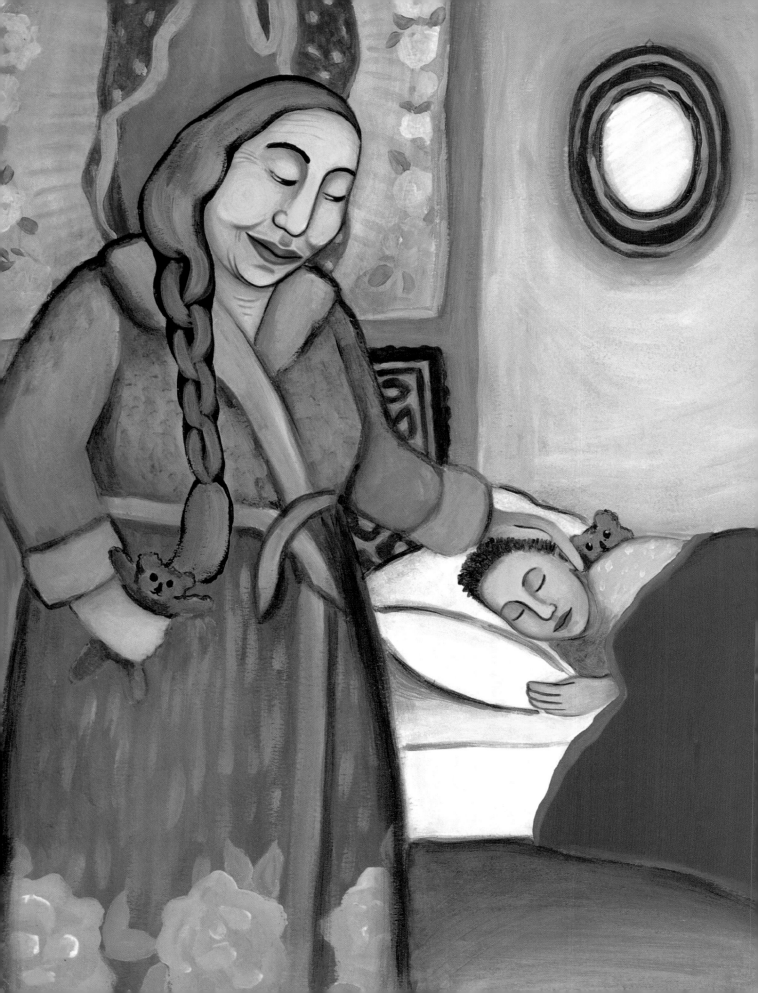

Oda a mis zapatos

mis zapatos
descansan
toda la noche
bajo mi cama

cansados
se estiran
se aflojan
las cintas

muy anchos
se duermen
y sueñan
con andar

recorren
los lugares
adonde fueron
en el día

y amanecen
contentos
relajados
suavecitos

Ode to My Shoes

my shoes
rest
all night
under my bed

tired
they stretch
and loosen
their laces

wide open
they fall asleep
and dream
of walking

they revisit
the places
they went to
during the day

and wake up
cheerful
relaxed
so soft

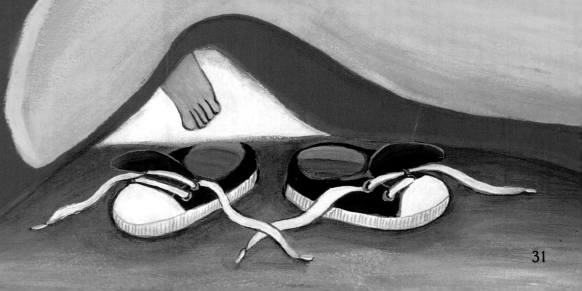

Afterword

My first memories of Mexico are from when I was four years old and I went with my family to visit our relatives in Jalisco, a state in western Mexico. Like many families heading south for vacation, we went by car, riding in my father's Pontiac station wagon. For me, Mexico was and still is an enchanted land where all senses come alive: colors are more colorful, tastes are tastier, and even time seems to slow down.

I spent many summer vacations in Atoyac with peasant relatives who led a simple and wholesome life. This collection of poetry is a celebration of this life when there were no radios or t.v. sets and the day's best entertainment came from the fantastic stories and incredible anecdotes told at night with the family seated around the kitchen table.   —Francisco X. Alarcón

Posdata

Mi primeras memorias de México son cuando tenía cuatro años de edad y fui con mi familia a visitar parientes que viven en Jalisco, un estado en el Occidente de México. Como muchas familias que van de vacaciones al sur, nosotros íbamos en coche, en la camioneta Pontiac de mi padre. Para mí, México era y sigue siendo una tierra encantada donde todos los sentidos se avivan: los colores tienen más color, los sabores tienen más sabor y hasta el tiempo parece que se dilata.

Yo pasé muchas vacaciones de verano en Atoyac con parientes campesinos que llevaban una vida sencilla y al mismo tiempo completa. Esta colección de poesía es una celebración de esta vida cuando no había radios ni televisores y el mejor entretenimiento del día eran los cuentos fantásticos y las anécdotas increíbles que se contaban por la noche con la familia sentada alrededor de la mesa de la cocina.   —Francisco X. Alarcón

Francisco X. Alarcón is an award-winning poet and educator. His acclaimed first book of poetry for children, *Laughing Tomatoes and Other Spring Poems*, received the National Parenting Publications Gold Medal Award and a Pura Belpré Honor Award from the American Library Association. The author of eight collections of poetry, Alarcón lives and teaches in Davis, California.

Maya Christina Gonzalez is a painter and graphic artist. Her artwork for her first award-winning collaboration with Francisco X. Alarcón, *Laughing Tomatoes and Other Spring Poems*, has been praised by reviewers as "upbeat," and "innovative," and "so bountiful it feels as if it's spilling off the pages." Gonzalez lives and frolics in San Francisco, California.